SACRED SONGS

BILL F. NDI

Langaa Research & Publishing CIG
Mankon, Bamenda

Publisher:
Langaa RPCIG
Langaa Research & Publishing Common Initiative Group
P.O. Box 902 Mankon
Bamenda
North West Region
Cameroon
Langaagrp@gmail.com
www.langaa-rpcig.net

Distributed in and outside N. America by African Books Collective
orders@africanbookscollective.com
www.africanbookscollective.com

ISBN-10: 9956-551-25-2

ISBN-13: 978-9956-551-25-5

Table of Contents

Dedication

To the humble servant of God, and prophet of our times, Prophet TB Joshua who has accepted and allowed the almighty God to use him mightily. To God be the glory and may the precious blood of His son Jesus Christ continue to cleanse this world from all sin.

LSS I

Why won't we Christian fellows feast on Hope?
We wait not at the short end of the rope
For ours is Faith built on a solid Rock
That flames and tempests from hell cannot rock.
And as the Temple? We know to be Christ
Who in us dwells and not the game of dice
Others toss and toil around with for Fun
And would march along to show their bright dress
Yet, when judgment day shall come they would run
While we, Synagogue brethren, shall not Stress;
Our foundation having been laid in Christ
The priceless commission we reap as prize!
Life without God, and without Christ? Don't take!
God and Christ are both our Icing and Cake!

LSS II

Our great world's a ship floating in the face
Of angry bitter waves left to menace
This ship overboard which we Christians stand
To let our hearts shine the light to the Land
With Lord's Mercy, Grace and Goodness graced
And grounded in His word with which we're braced
To break through darkness, storm and tempest
To mark this journey's end with Peaceful Rest
In the Lord's True Promise He sure does keep
With words given all sow what they reap
We start and end our journey in the Light;
Rile king of dark night to put up his fight
In vain attempt to sway us to his stow
Where in darkness we'd dwell down below.

LSS III

In my sleep with Him in mind I have peace
Yet, this world void of Him is torn apiece
And soaked in human blood that only stains
Where in the Righteous Blood I steep my pains
To come out pain-free with a Friend Jesus
In whose glossary Just Love abound no curse
Not even for they who with their axe break
His Sacred Heart. Yet, cannot His Love break;
His is steel solid for our Father's Love
Set no condition but fit us like a glove
Just the right size for the right hand fits well
When in His temple, we make place, He dwells
And makes our storms breeze we enjoy with joy
And have happiness nothing can destroy.

LSS IV

Your Spirit carnal men call foolishness
Knowing not they're dancing in pitch darkness
The Light you are shines the path to stride on
And come after You to the world beyond
Where in storms and tempest bring no sorrow
For all You swept and left bright tomorrow
For all whom their seeds in You do plant firm
Forfeiting all their pains never to squirm
For You'd wept for mankind and brought him grace
For which my pen shed its tears in Your praise
For the marvel and mystery that You've wrought
With none in human memory worth Your Worth
If Your Spirit they take for foolishness
My pen thus pleads with You for forgiveness.

LSS V

If our presidents' hearts were King size big
They would lay down their guns and give no fig
To ministers whose weapon is the Word.
Word or guns or words and guns would this world
A better home make for us passers-by
Here on earth in passing with will to vie
For earthly glory against that beyond
Which for our hearts gets ready a new dawn
For all prepared for life in a new home
Not the wanderers whose minds and souls streets roam;
Idling minds and souls to create an ideal
Workshop where the idler does his souls steal
Not when mind and soul on the Word focus
To steal the attention of their Divine Nurse.

LSS VI

Christ shed his Blood, wept, and cried for mankind
Yet, man's earthly dealings shows nothing so kind
With minds on high chair to drum each other
With songs of otherness far from order.
Like a tiger the strong hits hard the meek
And would say survival knows not the weak
Yet, the most high came in the lamb of Light
With great lessons, none of which about fight
For earthly grandeur, with one all seek first
The Kingdom in which we shall quench our thirst
Without any thoughts of this wilderness
Here on earth where those in power are mindless.
So, relent not for His Name's sake; stay strong
In mind and steer clear through you, comes no wrong!

LSS VII

Had He refused the cross, He'd have been death
And gone and left sick earth, without health,
Abounding in His Love, Mercies, and Grace
Unlike the fallen man's replete with craze
And refusal to stand up for the Cross
That has freed this world and left pain at loss
In which trade I'd rather join the winner
Should the cross be mine in the same manner
He went but lives on here to shine our path
For us to get home by-passing God's wrath
An instance none equals in their own tears,
Flesh, and blood in the way He's done to bless
Mortal man and sweep away all his stain
So, he stands a chance not to lose but gain.

LSS VIII

What is strange is that after our journey
We head home for rest where we'd never be
Garbed with toil and travail that'd been our plight
In a world of turmoil thrown in a fight
For gems none needs to take home when he'd leave
His trenches to head Home above this world
Around whose vicious circle Man's thought's whorled?
For sure to discount he'd one day take leave
Of his glittering flashes of hopelessness
Goading him to attempt to make useless
The Good Lord ready to turn a blind eye
For He's a Dad who sent His son to die
And keep our ocean of sin lucid clean;
Won't this suffice to make Dad's home our dream?

LSS IX

That commanded by God needs not spill blood!

His son He commanded to shed His Blood

And unchain us from the burden of wrong

In a world where tyrants would they prove strong

Thirsting after the blood of their fellow

Man who has his back turned not to fall low

Into the wrestle for things visible

But would he makes himself electable

Not to rule with ruthless and reckless swords

Which to describe call for more than just words;

To stand for election, one must have in

Hand everything above all, not a sin

He ought to have cleansed in the Holy Blood:

It's a sound design by our loving God!

LSS X

Crack not your door open to the devil
which in you, just like in grains, a weevil
Would deplete you of your sole quintessence
Outwardly he'd dress you with reverence
To masquerade your inner emptiness
And pride you shall flag in your foolishness
And turn up at the trumpet's sound uncouth.
Too late, there won't be a confession booth;
But for those ready it'll be a party
Long prepared as if awaiting, for tea,
A Great Guest of Honor with decorum
Whose coming like a thief's won't sound a drum!
Tie the loose ends and lie low to His will
And He'd raise you and ask you pay no bill!

LSS XI

It is just to be patient to the end
And in the Lord and with Him he won't bend
The Promise He has made in His good books
Yet, if you sway you will fall prey to crooks
Who'd plead for your good deeds and no belief
Or belief and no action: a mischief!
For His Voice is loud and clear as per faith
And action as a couple not their wraith.
Were experience the sacrifice? Gladly
Glimpse around! Point to the world what truly
You have that's yours and not by the Promise
From your birth through your life to your demise;
Where, when, and how did you make a preference
For where, when, and how He makes the difference!

LSS XII

Drum to the world how much you've accomplished
But like a dog if you have lived unleashed
Styling the Word for the insane, think twice
About the end and what you'd have as prize
For a life in the wild and with a brain
Sweeping your *raison d'être* down the drain
To give it the name of unrestrained choice
That guides you to all but not through the Voice
Now, take a step as in a dance, listen!
Hear your heartbeat and its music lesson!
Before you're blown up by joy that's short-lived
For you shall die and He won't be bereaved
For yours was overdose of disbelief.
By the Word with the Word secure relief!

LSS XIII

Why hurry when He who sets the pace herds?
Would you not head your flock as a shepherd?
What makes you think your creator goes to sleep,
Being your Shepherd, and would let stray His sheep?
You may want to run faster than His Light
Yet the Lord compares not with you His might.
Pace down and contemplate the world around
You'd see why once we claimed this world not round
Yet, before and after are His designs
And you shan't refute He showed you no signs
Which he has so done with road maps with routes
Sign posted which the sightless too can see
The abundance of His love void of fee
But which to have, you ought to be devout.

LSS XIV

With red milk of divine kindness He spread
On the cross and left his flesh to be bread
Broken by the broken to keep the bond
That in life they won't stray like vagabonds
But look up to the Most High everyday
Rather than look down on Him for no pay
Or have the world devoid of the Kingdom
In which love and peace composed are wisdom
All must have sown here on earth in advance
Not by projecting their own importance
But through acknowledgement of the Maker
Just as one would, toast in hand, a baker.
He changes the tides of various seasons
And all else unsaid, thus gives the reasons.

LSS XV

How, and to whom shall one make his case heard?
Having led our credit cross in the red
Our fingers won't point to others but us
For we'd filled our souls here on earth with pus
Instead of the milk of life that flows free
In the Word that bears fruits as would a tree
To feed both hungry poor and the wretched
Not the proud who would his pride like rocket
Project to summits to await his great fall
As would pride in its pride not heed the call;
Down to earth we'd hedge ourselves with hedges
Of His pledge that's never failed for ages
As was from then to date and from now on
We must be blest for He was of man born.

LSS XVI

Making detours on the way to Heaven
Colors the dreams of the owl and the raven
The one in the night thrives while the other
Like the night conceals dark secrets better
Unlike the Light by the Word thrown to shine
Our way on the stage where we'll never pine
Having been faithful now worthy of rest
In the home by the Lord for us made nest.
At every detour flag the courage high
And turn away from it never to sigh
Fortified by the Word, it shall be well
With you had you heeded the warning bell
And not stray like the beast further afield
But of the Word indeed make your true shield.

LSS XVII

Had the Lord thrown you deep down the valley,
Stoop to conquer both his grace and mercy
Both free for all who trust in Him in fact
And though the unruly won't face the fact
He gives them a leeway to change their stance
And not one to assert their ignorance
By thinking their distorted thoughts wisdom
Whence the real rest in seeking the Kingdom
With gate ready to open if we knock
To be welcomed for standing on the Rock
Of ages that changes not His bearing
For us to honor Him with thanksgiving
Not worth a fraction of the favor we
Enjoy together at home glad to be.

LSS XVIII

Fear not darkness! Fear the Light above all!
For fear of darkness some angels did fall
And would one took faith away from the Cross.
Braving both darkness and his night as dross
Is and should be the war we live to fight
And with our conquest we shall have no plight
After we've buried darkness in abysmal
Depth over which rectitude and moral
Fly a flag of wisdom in itself wise
Without which this journey takes home no prize
Yet, we know our labor shan't go in vain
For the Seed in us is the finest Grain
That would under rocks or in the desert grow
And shoot straight in the bone like the marrow.

LSS XIX

The Lord requests not much of us to know
Peace, love and compassion would make us Grow
Within these walls he built us as temple
One the enemy would see in shamble
After his failed rebellion against God
To whom our flesh and soul he wants at odd
Fraught with thoughts he may by this steal victory
And in fury drives home abject misery
Like the ill-wind with nothing good for man
Man has no choice in his heart but to ban
This outlaw who should not be allowed near
The temple of these virtues not for fear
But because where there's Light there's everything
To soothe and mend our souls left by the King.

LSS XX[1]

Some would tell you they know the date and time
The trumpet would sound; coming from what clime.
Convinced they may be! Yet, be not ripped off!
This is no news! You've been warned not to doff
Any hat for such madmen with sole goal
To defy and taint the Word with their coal
From the slaver's furnace mined with disgrace
And as the Truth sits up above, our face
Must turn to the Truth, look, in its eyes, straight
Without fear and embrace such gift of faith
When the sound comes all shall hear; plus the dead
And all prepared shall enjoy without dread
'Coz their Investment shall yield dividends
With neither twists nor turns. And, with no bends!

---

[1] This LSS was written on the night of the 27th June 2011 breaking June 28, 2011. And guess what, my step sister, Martha NDI, a fervent Baptist minister in one of the churches in Ngaoundéré Cameroon was killed by a thunderbolt. I have no doubt she was prepared for this day and her fate.

LSS XXI

Death you kill us humans. Shall you do same
With everlasting life that knows no blame?
Being ours we know for sure as God given
To us in this world by your greed driven
Of which you make human goal here on earth
Without those objects I'd glory at death
Yet, greed guides all thoughts to the outer self
With a show of possessions on the shelf.
What we need to leave behind in this world
Are not those but the feed groomed by the Word
To pave a way for the Foundation laid
By the Son of man who with His Life paid
The price that none on earth would pay without
Him who eternal life brings without doubt.

LSS XXII

Our life on earth is a part of a great gift
That some do take and would spend without thrift
Where carefulness authorized by the Word
Would scuttle humankind close by the Lord
Not that of the flies Golding holds down low
With his savagery and nothing as glow
To shine our way like the eyes of the lamb
Without which this life would have been a sham.
Thank His good name Man is not forever
Damned but given life that last for ever
Why can men not with gratitude say thanks
And not spend so much in killing with tanks?
This gift must not be by others stolen
But in unison shared as bread broken.

LSS XXIII

How would seeing Him help one determine
When disbelief has blown minds like a landmine
And all left of the minds is shattered bits
Of confused atoms that fall without wits
Where life in the Truth would stand top in form
And would itself reveal to stop the storm
Of lies intended for the destruction
Of the Word He inspired for instruction
And by and in which Word man is made free
Not to be on the same spot like a tree
But able to move to the left or right
And shoulder each other's burden; not fight
For delusions that shackle and drag down
In ways none sees he was going to drown.

LSS XXIV

Revel in evil and think it is life…
I would tell you, you do not have the knife!
Conceive my Father anything you would.
Mock Him not in the face, nor in the wood.
You have nowhere to hide for your inside
And your dark hidden secrets flank His sight
And make Him laugh loud at your childish prank
You think closely kept in a wooden plank
Box of vice you treasure at His expense
Remember life and death He doth dispense
And come His time you'd heave a big sad sigh;
Your award for dragging down the Most High
Won't you face the Truth? Revel in Beauty?
Loot His Love for you! Make it your booty!

LSS XXV

The package in which we're all wrapped is sin.
Yet, out we're free to leave it in a bin.
We need none to tell us to rid ourselves
Of the bright illusions that fill our shelves
At the sight of which we can't hold our breath
Where the Book tells us we need not just bread
For a life on earth wholesome holy whole
Which with heads against we shall score no goal.
We are blind thus far, not without a staff.
Use the one you have and take home a laugh
For the joys of laughter for you designed
From which fallen angels would you resigned
For them to have a big banquet in hell;
Yet, you'd heard the warning sound from the bell.

LSS XXVI

He holds the key to every door not us.

And to turn our backs on Him makes us worse.

Yet, before us is the line to follow

And not mock and laugh at Him to fall low

Priming over His Goodwill the evil

That would eat one from within like weevil;

To protect His seed we carry we must

Let Him move us as His wind does the dust

And cotton seed that would spring in the fields

And blossom to whiten gloom in the fields

It is His way not our way the right way

We need value to keep misery at bay.

Our Father does know the joys of our birth

And would we sailed through life with blissful mirth.

LSS XXVII

Just like a speck of dust lost in thin air
We see nothing run faster than a hare
Where our arbiter knows and sees all
And would with grace refuse to see us fall
For His is merciful cornucopia.
Here, our enemy would flash utopia.
With Him none finds himself at the cross road
Not even with inflicted pain as goad;
The truth with one lightens every burden
On the way to this Celestial Garden
In which one needs not a shroud to believe
At the end of it all He'd alone live
But one is free to embrace any doubt
But let not your doubts make you peacock proud.

LSS XXVIII

Never weight light the Almighty's power
It does rain blessings to keep our flower
Fresh and bright so all eyes can on it land
While we sing His praises playing a band
All the Time for He is good and gracious
To hand down tableaux of life so precious
That many a doubting Thomas won't brace
Till they have witnessed for themselves His Grace
Abounding in the fact of them alive
With life he could decide to them deprive
For His goodness is constant and won't yield
To depravity bringing no proceeds
He has given all the choice to follow
His only Son and be saved or fall low.

LSS XXIX

My mind led me by the hand to the village
In which yesteryears death was not of age
And his ill-wind hit twice or thrice a year
And now that of age he's become, we hear
No! We come close to him by the minute
And would not leave alone endless dispute
That like weevil eats up the frail fabric
Of a foundation once laid not with brick
But this milk of human kindness taken
And spilled here and there to leave Man broken
And hardened only to be transported
Still by the hand of fate negotiated
By the Father's will and for the Great Love
He has for the broken who would play tough.

LSS XXX

The strength of the flesh shows not the inner
Who should wheel from inside like a driver
Whose achievements want in glory to God
And need be given Him for room and board
For what is worldly that's not celestial?
Not even the beauty that's palatial
Adorning those we would leave on earth
Onto which fools do cling for fear of death
Where the wise would fear only God for life,
This one on earth with transience that is rife.
With God behind you? For sure, life is yours!
He won't fail! He is both day and night nurse!
His loving and soothing hands would caress
Just you intimately without recess!

LSS XXXI

Treat His might with spite. You'll be broken.

For you'd been forewarned and you won't hearken.

Follow His path and to glory he'd shine

Your way through caring not you were sand blind

And blind to proofs he had shown you and just

You and brought in broad daylight with no dust

To soil the glitter of such a marvel

All could see if their heads they had level

And not attempt to project false wisdom

With allegiance to outrageous kingdom

In which no peace reigns and pains take new life

Whereas on His path one rides to New Life

In which Peace reigns and Pains are interred;

Why won't this be the Kingdom most preferred?

LSS XXXII

God's recipe to man is obedience!

Yet, man garbs himself with disobedience

In hope he peace of mind and happiness

Finds with his back turned against God's goodness;

Without cause loving the things he's chosen

Over the simplest task ever given

To a *homo erectus* that is free

To believe all will run dry not the sea

Of God's gracious good love to man; His Son

He sent us as Light that outshines the Sun

He's my take I choose over the dark knight

Whose fall from grace by his quest for might 'light

My devotion to the Son must endure

For he shines my path to the grand treasure.

LSS XXXIII

God knows and sees what you and I do not
And He and only He'd bring us to naught
In all our vain attempt to short change Him
Knowing not we're blighting the sweetest dream
He wishes for us and we for ourselves
Would rather go for those things on the shelves
Which in turn, would in their own right lead us
To our doom in which we'd be worse than pus
Which I know you don't want to be though proud
In your stead with arrogance that sings loud,
Louder, the loudest song of ignorance
To project the stench of putrid fragrance
You would my world lift as the essential
When I know and doubt not the celestial.

LSS XXXIV

Wait for this world to change not on the Lord
You'd have no life and would be really bored
Not what He designed for you with True Love
That is boundless with splendor that's not rough
Pick up your courage and hit the one road
On which he set you free t'expect no goad
Raining pain on your back for you to stay
In the herd you think foolish for they pray
Yet, you know with pangs of hunger you need
His mercy for the rains to grow your seed;
If you ask not for sure on the seed mould
Would grow and you would have vanquished the gold
He'd in store for you and of your making
I won't stand you chide my heavenly King.

LSS XXXV

We make mistakes, drown in them and blame God
When in our lives we strive to show He's naught
Which for real we are without Him above
Looking after poor us with ceaseless Love
All the bling blings of this world shall not buy
Yet, we would refuse to stop and ask: "why?"
Hoisting our ego so high; blind to fall
That would be so great at His trumpet's call
Which call I fear not for 'biding by Him
And following the light that does not dim
With Christ in me my path I follow through
The thorns erected to instill in you
Great fear which one needs not with the Winner
By his side victory's mold is a primer

LSS XXXVI

A Society without leaders is worse
Not as a world without God and at loss
Like a home without a head with its void
That won't be filled by an army deployed
So is a church without Christ doomed to fall
And never to get up on its feet tall
To face the angel of fall who finds joy
With attempts to bury the Truth, his ploy
For our knowledge of this Truth paves the way
To stay us away from going astray
To pump his anger as we make it home
Home sweet home filled with joy and far from Rome
At gain with undeserved mercies and grace
That's in sooth the reason to sing His Praise!

LSS XXXVII

Undeserved favor from the Lord's mercy
We are given and we still fail to see
The greatest gift of His grace grow and glow
With flourishes of free air He bestows
And free of charge even to the defiant
Who at the top of his voice breeds miscreant
In attempt to defy a simple rule
With Haughtiness and claims he plays it cool.
I would take the heat and stick to the Books
And not play by the laws of hardened crooks
Whose mirrors in the sun reflect to blind
Those eyes wrapped up with things deep down the mine
And far from these minds with blossoms of peace
And unwrapped arms to hug the Prince of Peace.

LSS XXXVIII

With the seed of God in me, my nursery
Grows seedlings that would be void of worry
And loudly sing the beauty of the Lord
Soothing the heart with no place for the sword
So much my dream for every heart to be
This nursing bed of roses before me,
The treasure before which I hail His Name
So great that I can avoid to take blame
For things I could handle without pressure
Yet, enticed by mares of mundane pleasure
Headiness would incubate to freeze free
Will we're called upon to delight in free
And harvest its plentiful juicy fruit
We have, hold and find of astute repute.

LSS XXXIX

Let them fly rockets to the outer space
He knew the Bible would get him a place
By the Lord the maker of the universe
And the sheen of trinkets would not reverse
The flow of his zeal to follow the course
He turned to in trouble times for recourse
As his mission he accepted with knowledge
They'd attempt to push him over the edge;
His Trust and candor stood by the Master's
Will requesting he followed His orders.
Jerry, the faithful General remains
That soldier whose cries never were in vain
As vain as the palace he'd not accept
To inherit over his God's precept.

LSS XL

Christ builds us with bricks of our failure.
With crumbs of success we build our failure.
Priding ourselves great architects at work
Strong of head to acknowledge Christ, the Rock
On which the broken lean to stand erect
Behind their Guide and His course that's direct;
What makes men to think themselves above all
And fail to see they're on the brink of fall
That would come one day come rain come sunshine
And they would have their pride put on the line
And that won't be for the thrill or the joy
For our victory shall have their pride as toy
Not worth the time to fiddle around with;
Both them and theirs that reside in the heath.

LSS XLI

Human wisdom would lead one off the tract
Whereas Prayers would get one there intact.
Feel free to despise all, not the Power
In the Word rooted that like a tower
Soars up in the Heavens and wrought marvels
Before one's eyes with no need for travels
To see sight labeled wonders of this world;
That's the spin they would we our time with whirled.
Yet, the light in us would put out such spin
And still lead us through life through thick and thin;
Out-marveling the wonders of their fancy
Dream world of bald-faced inhumanity,
Give the world her wisdom and stick to your
Word of prayer and up above you'd soar.

LSS XLII

Live and let's laugh with and not at our God
Who does the world wrought and would bring to naught
The haughtily bawdy with their giggle
And judgments that do their thinking tickle
In their deep slumber in which they sleep walk
With their free self-indulgence in cheap talk
That won't stand to face the Lord of Judgment
For fear His ruling would make them lament
And sit tight lips before this raging wrath
Given they, on their journey, strayed the path
To the glorification of Divine
Judge who now cast them into the ravine
Where they thought they'd buried us forever
Knowing not our Great Judge had signed: Never!

LSS XLIII

Won't you rather be the scum of this earth
Like Christ crucified for His Sacred Heart
So pure a Heart that paint and taint won't hold
Onto the way man clings tight onto gold
And be the jewel your maker treasures
Or the rod with which he others measures
Or would you continue to spit on Love
Sane and free for no fee with none to scuff
This sweet smooth scented garden at your feet
That throws the enemy into a feat?
In your shoes I would heed His Sacred Heart
And show His foes how Love flows from His Heart
The home in which dwells and works forgiveness
That sets mankind free from his pettiness.

LSS XLIV

God led me to the Synagogue whose light
Does shine the way to our broken souls bright;
With mercy and grace which many a man
His ingratitude flags and would demand
God's Head. This? He's boldly done on the cross
Through His Son who spilled His blood so precious
Not to stain but cleanse cleaner than clean;
And bring home such health on which we are keen
To stitch the filthy rags we have become
In our vain fight to break His giant calm
Without which He'd have joy to have a laugh
With us in sight broken without a staff
Yet, His boundless Love overflows to sooth
And balm the hearts of heathens so uncouth.

LSS XLV

Lord, thank You for these eyes that see beyond
The physic which holds many as its bond
And enslave their thoughts with such stale image
Which on them enthrones its weighty luggage;
To leave their hidden inner thoughts all crushed
Whence mine, at Your feet, by Your mercy crushed
Revel with joy to fill human hearts full
With sights of Kindness from your merciful
Well of wellness I greet with thankfulness
The heathen would reject for godlessness
And wish to see a heart sore for no pay
As all he knows is to lead men astray.
Yet, Your Son is my Way, my Truth and Light
That doth avail to all and without pride.

LSS XLVI

Myself, I insulate with Lord Jesus!
Faith's the gateway of life for the righteous!
Let the Lord as fire consume your soul whole
And joy with His wrath than accept their dole
As He from the ashes of a burn fire
Endows a phoenix with wings that will fly
Not just one for desertification
But His Truth's that thrives in every nation
For all to reap ripe fruits of faithfulness
He grows for all on His tree of goodness.
Mine, I do harvest and so enjoy them
And my heart overflows with seeded gem
So smooth that no stone roughens him by touch
Nor by hard knocks to hear me scream out ouch!

LSS XLVII

Beautiful winged cherub I would I hugged;
You lift me high, high up as would no drug
And up in my head you fly without end
Bringing joys of the Word: "world without end"
And my ears would never fatigue to drink
From such fountain of life where my thoughts sink
In you with hope these thoughts meet Truth and Love
In Gracious abundance and not tough love
For the Lord builds no bridge where not needed
As he showed me you need not be dreaded
I laid my head on the Bible for God
To tell me my labor of love won't rot
Or if my love's measuring rod you'd be
But of the painful beestings He rid me!

LSS XLVIII

Filthy rags we have become in His eyes
Yet, His goodness listens to our cries
These rumbling cries all human ears won't hear
Like God hears all silent cries with one ear
And doth assures we need not harbor fright
For He is full fair aware of our plight
And come His time which often is the best
On a gold platter He would serve us Rest
That's not for those who for the sake of doubt
Would doubt and question His ways with a pout.
As a rag make yourself ready for use;
Judicious instrument God won't misuse
For He so does caringly till the end
In this life so smooth and straight without bend.

LSS XLIX

A brethren has just been elected home
And my heart twitched I were the coxcomb
But the voice in won't let me taint the Word
For no place is better than by the Lord
Who life instills and decides when it ends
Whether in it one plods, treads, tramps or wends
On the path He had blazed from inception
With a follow up through to conception
And the unfolding of the cute bundle
Whose election does awake our rumble
In the flesh that has fallen short of fame
Since the first Man and wife gave in to shame
So shall peace only come with eternal
Rest that makes of enemies fraternal.

LSS L

Burst not my balloon of Godliness

Jimmy Cliff went to Nigeria

They would shame on him did rain

Here I am at Tuskegee

Where my love would she made me get shamed

For I feel for her God fearing mind;

And yes! I told her I care for her

Even added that I love her

Yes! My neighbor she was by the good books

Yet, her mind I saw fly sky high

With me projected a pervert

Whence my soul I lift to God

And would with it on earth I rot

Than be clad in robes of her dream pervert

LSS LI

My empty closet is filled with God's Love!
Others fill theirs with bones to prove they're tough!
Tough, are they really? I'm still to think so!
Aren't they stunted and never will grow?
Aren't they at loss without His glory?
Or do they glory to get in History?
Maybe, these skeletons, mute as they are,
Never will stand to leave a tale ajar
Like mine wide open with a coarse voice to stop
Human skinning and scheming from the top
Where resides, with joy to play, the enemy
Who closes up to sting as would a bee
Whose deeds bring to mind none of its produce
But guise of same malevolence they traduce.

LSS LII

Lift yourself above all but forget not
Were you not the Lord's instrument, you're naught
And such an empty tank car with no fuel
Or such monsters whose thoughts and deeds are cruel!
Cruel? You might ask: what does it mean?
Backing your misdeeds the Lord has washed clean
With his travails through the various stations
He borne with courage to bring salvation
To your breed that has chosen but a fall
In self pride and material to stand tall
Before dwarfs whose crime has been to look up
To a father so dear who's given up
His only pride of fatherhood, His Son
Who'd shed His blood to make joy sheen like sun.

LSS LIII

Death, I once told you, you make me laugh
And you poked fun of me and called me daft
Then sneaked in my garden and stole my Rose
Hopeful sadness feeds me an overdose
Of your earthly garden jam packed with thorns
Out of which was made a crown to be worn
And borne by Christ who promised he'd be in
Paradise with all who had let him in.
So, my smile you broaden for I do know
For sure where my Rose is kept, she shall grow
As she had in this life with the Lord God
And if you thought I'd be dragged in the mud
I would tell you in this game I have won
With a giggle that will never be worn.

LSS LIV

Caesar, you're caught on your way to manhood
By death, master of that owl, sent to hoot
His telltale sign of your hasty journey;
One you embraced for your call of duty
Now you are gone! The vacuum can't live on
For where we had played and at times did run
As children do under the rain showers
Of blessings God poured on them as ours was
And now inscribed on my traveling mind
As your sacred name "Sing and Drum" for the blind
I don't need the material you to know
God the father wanted it to be so
And so I greet the bird of the dark night
Who'd propelled you to your stead as a knight.

LSS LV

And you say you're an angel! With owls wings?
You dare want to pass it for chicken wings
And must have molded in your mind a fool
Whose knowledge of his Maker beats the rule
Were you attentive, you'd know am not one
For, with my Master I shall not be wan
With my eyes up to Him and down on you
Why shan't I listen to songs from the cuckoo?
Sweet tender songs to sleep lulling my heart
With warmth yours never will spark from your hearth
He is up above and rains me showers
And I sleep soundly with dream of flowers
Void of thorns you used to crown my savior
In hope I'd fear and change my behavior

LSS LVI

Unfold those big bundles with shapes and shades
In which you come and I'll name you the spades
With which you tempted my Lord on the mount
I'll then make your smokescreen ship go aground
With my grip firm on His Grace and Mercy
Relishes which with zest I do make merry
Which in turn corrode your crumpled forehead
As your aspiration is pronounced dead
By my tenacity to repay you
Your callousness not with heartlessness too,
A sap that leaves your ocean of vengeance
In which you delight in your arrogance
And vain attempt to stick yourself above
Children whose breath from heaven comes with Love!

LSS LVII

By you I stand both in words and in deeds
For others' words may fly as well as deeds
My words and deeds' wings and feet I have cut
For both to be firm and but thee no but
For my mouth ate You, Bread and won't let woe
Through it on Your saintly body stone throw
You in me, must I breathe humility
For by Yourself You are my reality
Crooked tongues would You were but a figment
With which tongues some waste time in argument
Arid and fruitless like a desert shrub
With passion burning to Your victory rob
Such thirst does not but beckons my disdain
For the same who trust not for them you're slain.

LSS LVIII

In my seeking journeys I hear you Lord
In the silence of my world without word
Telling me as does Your good books: You are
That which was before the birth of the star
That would shine the way through all hoops and loops
By the meanest foe placed in guise of scoops
To have fools' hearts pounding with mundane joy
When they have all but failed to see his ploy.
Yes, Lord! I hear you! Thus, let my pen run
And embrace this paper not just to pun;
A play not advised with the greatest Word
That spells nothing else but Your might Lord
Behind which all must line without questions
The like of Thomas who doubts and questions.

LSS LIX

Hopping out of bed from a deep slumber
I revisit the dream, a light lumbar
Above and for me placed to delight in
My Creator with knowledge I would win
Against all odds the foe mounts on my path
To see me fall in his pool for a bath
With such blood stained water he has boiled hot
And left for fools to wallow in and rot.
This, the foe takes for his smoothened wisdom;
A trap to stop sane minds from the Kingdom
Not only promised in the good old books
But preached by the Lord who warns against crooks
Who themselves in cassocks of faith now cloak
To fool the world theirs is faith made of oak.

LSS LX

Eyes will drink at you with amorous me
In dreams in the land of milk and honey
Of which your sweetness is manifold blessed
By Him who knows and frees us from stressed
Untimed life in this world the devil would
He ruled all human flesh with his owl's hoot;
But God has glazed our love with honesty
No amount of frowns would render silly
Not even with the hate spelled on your face
I forgive for myself not for your craze
Of carnal desire to drag men's soul down
The mire as you would you saw them drown
Now, let your beauty embrace this blessed love
And savor His sweetness never enough.

LSS LXI

Riches of this world is the rag of time
Knowledge of the Lord is the song I chime
And know I, not all would to its tune dance
For the Lord summons all to take a stance
Notwithstanding their season, clime and tide
For He leaves none in the dark without light
And even sent His Son to shine the way
To follow for He is the only way
Not the fast lane which we know to Hell leads
And on which no bells ring to break in bits
The chimera which like shadows men chase
In their vain attempt to escape the mace
Hovering over their heads till their demise,
A price they pay to the Lord they despise.

LSS LXII

Impute your woes on me… Would you do same
When comes that last day you would for your shame
Answer before the Justice of judges
Who strengthens me never to bear grudges?
You have heard my question and may not see
Any answer from you is worthless flea
With which my mind needs not itches nor yens
To strike it a deathblow scripted in pens
Held by human hands so with blood sullied
After you had in your mad rage bullied
Meek and weak us forgetting in the lamb
The Light of this world outshone any lamp
And lives to shine even dead on the Cross
And before Him you shall tremble like dross.

LSS LXIII

I crack open my blanket in the morning
The like of rose flowers their way cracking
Out of their sepals for a new dawn God
Has blessed them with not to drag in the mud
His holy name but glorify such bright
Sunny day freely given with no fright
To watch out for but bask in this freedom
Men seek and won't find in earthly kingdoms
In the mornings as he knock on my door
And I remember how wretched and poor
My day would be were I not to answer
This gentle and inviting knock, softer
Than a comforting cotton comforter
Which is normal for the Lord's my answer.

LSS LXIV

These thoughts and feelings crawled into my bed
And with me won't sleep if for Pascal's bet
I took the mighty potter who with clay
Instilled the first breath of life in a day
And has many, many days given Man
For no pay but quest to obey demands
He'd inscribed on stone as His commandments;
Our abode by which would bee sweet condiments
Honey's sweetness would not even second
In the land of milk and honey fecund
Tabled to Man as writ of things to come
When he follows this just path to go home
To eternal rest in tranquility
The upright embrace for eternity.

LSS LXV

My God's Love is mine on which heathens tread
With spite he for their souls does provide bread
And calls the shots that bring calamity
On them that sing self-importance worry
Free and think Him a figment from no lobe
Created to seat and feed some famished pope
Whose only source of solace is to garb
Himself with robes and go around to grab
Specs of gilt dust from the poor mine dwellers
Who must their soot forfeit to new settlers
With habitual drive that wants to defy
The designed order met here as reply
To God of humility here on earth.
He shall sure riposte in the end with death!

LSS LXVI

I'd be a big fool to conceive the breath
Of life in me the sole wrought of the bread
Made with man's unclean hands with sin soiled!
I'd indeed be letting my fervor foiled
And at a cost to make my Lord not proud
Though He would care less one followed the crowd
For He is all mercy and grace unbound
Saying why my ink His glory resound
And color sheets with calls He's the purpose
Of life here on earth and bright as a rose
That tickles both our eyes and our senses
To uphold His honor with reverences
On the path with arrows to victory land
Pointing to the savior's stretched helping hand.

LSS LXVII

My dream I'd cling onto and rather die
Than let go to garb my stomach with pie
My Lord warns we need not live by alone
And I won't be the first to throw a stone
At a counsel that grounds my faith in God
For fragile pleasures that drag in the mud
The Word words cannot a picture of make
And which will mouths water and fill than cake
With which steam in the brains the flames won't die
For the heart hears a cry; not a far cry
With the Lord of hosts heading an army
To make of my dreams the flag of loyalty
Who has never slipped from Job till today
Even when some would he bagged vice as pay.

LSS LXVIII

Lord, your fire burns me not but caresses
My soul and starts this wind that goads senses
Away from that juncture one would he clang
And clang onto a world with open fang
Ready to shred your artistry with poise
The world has in display with a loud noise
That would demolish the drums of my ear
As would a woodpecker wood without fear
Where I revel in your honor and trust
And would with delight be returned to dust,
Thoughts that for others burn hotter than hell
'Coz their journey's end on earth tolls the knell
To eternity after which glory
For you is this song I sing for victory.

LSS LXIX

My big bag of love is what I carry
And to the world you muse that I carry
A big bag of lust after your tulip
Running to come steal a kiss from your lip
With my love virtue cast into this mold
Our story however will still be told
In words that would caress some eager ears
Even when you've shut my mouth with your fears
Fears you need not frequent for mine's thorn free
And has been so set by Christ Jesus free
With the oneness of humankind upheld
I'd hug any from the steppes to the Veldt
'Coz Christ the Light like the Sun for all lives
So we can abide and wield olive leaves.

LSS LXX

Our God plucked the fruit of love from its tree
And for love gave us its seed to be free
And free to carry Him with us at will
And to pave the way for His name to kill
Our ills were we to stand firm by His Name
Which the meandering plague plays with but a game
And with blindfold have the weak heart pump low
In the poisoned tree from which he fell low
And retained that such folly to claim fame
With which he obscures all else but his Shame
The way for the world to rebound after
And blight our journey to the hereafter.
Yet, with the seed of love in us we'll thrive
And will in the sea of life to come dive!

LSS LXXI

Lord's wisdom brews not a pot of hemlock
But plods in with age that comes to unlock
The chains of worldly tidings wherein swims
Man's skewed vision fallen prey to the whims
And caprices of the fallen angel
Who in his lies now glories as devil
Whose refracting mirage leads to darkness
Which darkness reveals his venture hopeless.
Let the vapor of the Lord's brew the fog
That covers the mountain of your good work
From roaming and raging hounds hunting down
The young light in you with both grin and frown
In their lightless light only by the Light
Outshone with sole goal to make our stay bright!

LSS LXXII

Sing glory to the Lord and shame his foe
Who with ruse would bring you no reign but woe
In which he wallows and would you follow
His way to brag and fall far, far below
Where the Lord would we lie not to ourselves
But stand by the truth He is; not on shelves
Where trinkets glitter as lure to dead brains
Who in life see only material gains
In stead of salvation borne on the cross
With throbbing pain and bleeding blood not pus
Up to which we must look for help and grace
When our enemy draws us to disgrace.
These little sacred songs for glory sing
To the one and only almighty King.

LSS LXXIII

He snaps His finger! A cry becomes a smile!
His hand to the sick and poor on a mile
Long queue stretched cures and blooms flowers of health
On His highway paved with wisdom's sheath
For man to close his eyes 'n bow in honor
For the Lord's never seen on street corner
Yet, of the world he doth make his foot rest,
And of any heartbeat choose its arrest.
So, the music my heart plays glorifies
The Name besides which man's would attract flies
Such as those Golding make of man their lord
One with brain driving to uphold a sword
Whose sharp blade won't cut a drop from a pen
In the hand of just one Lamb and not ten.

LSS LXXIV

Some would they saw God to swallow their pills
Yet, unseen, He's the banker who pays bills
Even those of the bankrupt who with spite
Will spit and puke at His name that makes them
Tremble for His is but a glowing gem,
Ruby red heart he sent to die for man
So ungrateful to stand and reprimand
A fellowman for standing by the light;
Our Lord knows we'll by it stay till His call
And will brave the foe till we see him fall
And fall he'd fall and fall in his dark pit
To rock the butt of worldly gain he'd lit;
And the silence of our hearts will heave cries
Of our victory for our Lord never dies!

LSS LXXV

Call Him fake! That bait I would not take!

Make your peace by craving all that's fake

And to your face I will sing to you

Without fear you are a shame times two

For you trample underfoot His Name

Free of stain with thoughts and claims of fame

And knowing he does not His work do

For such as to His faith He is True

As I hold fast to my refusal

Of mud slings at my divine royal

From you or any who with putrid

Slurs try to drag down the slums and rid

My world of light shining from His Heart

To guide my steps for He's my shepherd.

LSS LXXVI

When we choose to glue to the rules, no games!
And should we play fair we'd shoulder no blames
And never turn around to point fingers
At the poor and feeble whose thought lingers
Far, far away from the hot pit of doom
Yet doth do by daily truth near the tomb
The Lord hath ordained as way to freedom
For by dying they're heirs to the kingdom
Whence Dives his on earth had arrogated
And drenched in not-to-be celebrated
Greed which ushered him yonder his playground
Leaving the ship he rocked and rocked aground
For the Word does not lie and would not sleep
'Cos the Word's a good guide herding His sheep.

LSS LXXVII

With the Word I feed my soul full
Where others see in me a fool
The spirit in me is the sage
That came first to mention an age
To come when man shall his creator
Treat with spite, scorn, and arrogance
And make himself being of importance
And make his creator a mere spectator.
Yet, Master maker is the sole breaker
And breaks when He wills just as He would soothe
And balm aches and pains even of my tooth
And has He always brightened my bleaker
And somber nights and makes me accept your scorns
For Christ my pains borne with your crown of thorns.

LSS LXXVIII

I shall let the blood of Jesus rain down
From my pen and let others for a clown
Take me; which clown I am won't wear a frown
For with a smile I've always made my crown
Like Christ of pains made His of thorns for me
And turned my bitter tears into honey
Sweet, sweet honey with no sting from a bee
That my view shades with the splendor I see
As was never before seen in time past
And I will not wait till the die is cast
And make it slippery in sooth to hold fast
To Him as I do this day till the last
When I my Lord obey and bite the dust
Happily as I mock your mundane lust.

LSS LXXIX

Lord, let not the devil tempt me this man
Of God cleansing this weird world is not one
And thank you that far cry from outside came
And not from within as it did for Cain
As I would rather like Abel be slain
Than live and replicate Cain's claim to fame.
Lord, give me the courage to brave the fiend
Whose duplicities lead him to my friend
And parents poisoning them in the head
That my quest for you would leave them bloodshed
As he knows I won't soil my hands in blood
As I'd rather on my back take their rod
As I seek sanctuary in your bosom
For with you, I'd need to pay no ransom.

LSS LXXX

Do not be tempted by such lights that blind
And leave you in darkness and in a bind
As they litter the streets and project flesh
To set you on fire to craving it fresh
Only to steal you away from the Light
That never would put up a fight for might
For it holds in it the Way and the Truth
Which if you should follow would only sooth,
Calm, and shine your passage through the rough sea
Of life we'd need the lamb's blood to be free
As freely we were made and born not by
Chance in this world people think they can buy
Their ticket through and ignore the Maker
Providing us with bread like a baker.

LSS LXXXI-a

Blind me to my royal robes of this world
Let me dwell not in them to let this word
From my pen flowing, flow to lead the mind
Away from the one who's nothing but kind
And indeed to give up life for my kind
To live and constantly the world remind
The Lamb not lion, wolf or tiger the world
Runs and does so without using a sword
I need not to stress my nobility
Into which I was made to be born free;
And now their world with its dark lightless light
Attempts to push me into a nameless fight
To which I have my back against and would
Never retreat as they wish to the wood.

LSS LXXXI-b

The world crashed on me with wish to tie me
Down thinking not His name would set me Free
And now Free, my face with a smile adorned
Nods at their lightweight and pride still not dawned
On them for they're too blind to see this pit
By the enemy dug for them to sit
And wallow in their mess and heap the blame
On the poor soul whose sole dream is the Name
That has no blame and does not lame at all
For, in the end, he would on earth stand tall
To tell the world its weight on the poor erred
And didn't see it would have His anger flared
And turned the human world up-side-down
And would lift me up and not let me down.

LSS LXXXII

How do I dare sculpt wholesome holiness
For mind so Neolithic to grasp the mess
Man brought himself into with chants of gore
Leaving the bath that has since become lore
To the bruised and battered left in the pool,
The pool of blood in which, forced by this fool,
They squirm like worms in his underworld, not theirs
Yet, herein, their triumph shall come without spears
For theirs is the strongest hand that shields them
And would welcome them home with an anthem
Piped from the trumpet of the Lord of Host
For whom they fasted without any toast
For their life depended not on their strength,
Which strength could not take them halfway the length.

LSS LXXXIII

In the chaos of God's world, there is order
Which accepts all and makes none the other
In theirs ordered with lawless disorder
Which leaves our kind pushed into the farther
Fringes of the stolen gold covered lanes
Knowing not God would uncover their stains
Which they would like transported on our trains
To collide us head on to sit and smirk
As they leave the burden on our poor clerk
Good old clerk Woolman who points to their ilk
The trouble with having you and me in
Servitude while blind to the light within
Shining our way to God-given oneness
In which we will never know any mess.

LSS LXXXIV

Lord our God, thank you for my given faith
For, 'tis the rampart that shields from the fate
Befalling many moaning men on earth
Whose life's depth and breadth show nothing but dearth
Of the quintessence of your grand design
From which with might man would rather resign
Blind to the fact that choices he makes borne pain
At first sight shining bright with beams of gain.
With your gift to me Lord, with smile I beam;
And the joy I have men won't know in a dream.
By your gift I stand and would with your name
In my heart make a brand that'd soar all fame
Earthly fame men would die for, oblivious
'Tis a construct of that foe who's devious.

LSS LXXXV

As the clock ticks by I know to my death
I'm close with joyful heart far from the heath
The foe of my soul would he dragged me in
With his bait that always leads man to sin
Sin, which only dimwit fools venerate
To their own detriment, does triplicate
Their woes and drive a nail into the coffin
One in which is buried fools' endorphin.
The Word hints a word to a wise enough
To ease the life of all who from the trough,
By the Lord provided, drink at its source
As God is for them Reference and Resource
That hedges and shields them in misfortune
Which foe and kin would exploit as fortune.

LSS LXXXVI

Brand yourself what you will without His will
Your toing and froing will be uphill
From which your pride will slip and slit its throat
Before your eyes which will fill a moat
When you had the choice to seek the Lord's grace
Your thoughts went to dare taunt Him with disgrace
Yet, in His infinite mercy, you're spared
And given time to turn coat and be geared
Towards homecoming to roost like the fowls
Not the hungry feline that in the fields prowls
Prodding your lascivious drive after flesh
And such drive needs not but the Word to quench
Its burning furnace fanned and flamed from hell.
Remember, with the Word all shall be well!

LSS LXXXVII

Lord when you snatched me from the mouths of wolves,
Wolves cursed the day they refused to evolve
With desire to be knaves to fallen
Angels with dreams full to leave me broken
Yet you know as always who sticks his gut
For Your Name so Holy that none can hurt
And sneak away without a slip and fall
Unlike those who exalt Yours to stand tall
Against the wall erected between us
I will sing my sacred song filled with pulse.
This silence of Your voice sounds the trumpet
That invites all to inter the hatchet
And reject that beast of the underworld
Who by no means shall rule over Your world.

LSS LXXXVIII

I have no reason to cry for Christ wept
And my pains, woes, and sorrows were all swept
And buried far from the shores of my bliss
Where I rest and never hear the snake hiss
And waste no time to think the world random
Creation and be made to pay a ransom.
Why worry when I need to stay and trust
In Him and He will give me more not rust
To live for and be freer with my heart,
His dwelling, within which he warms like hearth?
Don't you think I'd be a fool for dwelling
In this world and not make me His dwelling?
I'd rather not thirst after your freedom
For it keeps me away from the Kingdom.

LSS LXXXIX

Angel of death you might haunt me in dreams
But I will not for your sake utter screams
For by His light I stand not your darkness
In which with your dark light you birth sleaziness
If you wish, come as a brother alive
Or dead and that would still not be the drive
To make me scream for I know you are naught
Which to crack would never be a hard nut
As long as I have the bounds well defined
To leaving your rugged plane undermined
As with His right hand a pen I grip firm
To spew ink on paper and make you squirm
Each time His words in prints are vocalized
To bury with it your dream of being idolized.

LSS LXXXX

My physique I know mortal not my soul
Blessed by the Lord my God to live life whole
And be covered by the blood of the Lamb;
Meek little lamb outshining every lamp
Would, out of Love for me, be sacrificed:
Prize with which I would not be apart prised
And on my soul engraved like commandments
Feeding me full with pious achievements.
The vultures of this world aim at my flesh
When the Lamb by grace doth my soul refresh
To lighten the load weighted by vultures
Who in our practices see strange cultures
For the Lamb herd the lions in their weakness
Heeding the Lamb to guide with His meekness.

LSS LXXXXI

There's one and only one infiniteness.
Man's refusal and ignorance won't make
A dint on His infinite righteousness
Not even when His enemy would fake,
Tempt, and drag weak men in the dark of night
With false promises they would be made knights;
Knights working in the dark who're full with mischief
And serve none but him that's the thief in chief
Leading such thugs to stilling given joy.
Onto mine, I hold fast and heed not the ploy
He brandishes after me. I refuse
His urge and talk of wisdom both refuse
That won't even serve as manure for weeds
Where the Lord's goads indeed towards good deeds!

LSS LXXXXII

Man's machinery disappoints him but not you
Lord who would stretch your hands to the poor too
And heal and make sure he who endures pain
So does by his own reckless choice for gain
Gain which will tempt and blind to the essence
Of life above which you're the quintessence
That rocks my world with treasures that elate
And spurs my run towards you as my date
And my date you will never fail to save
My rooted soul which the foe would enslave.
My root dipped deep in faith bright with Light sips
From the fountain that always wets tulips
Whose flower the dove on its beak brought home
To tell this world is far away from home.

LSS LXXXXIII

Engulf me in your Holy Ghost fire
And these songs I sing won't need a lyre
To please listening ears that after truth thirst
To know in their quest that you are the first
And hold the last word which on sand written
Shall not be erased and shan't be beaten
By the air you choose to breathe in a mold
And cast you craft and don't leave in the cold
For the love, care, and grace you show broken
Men who, for their wicked ways have fallen
Into shame and disgrace, now seeking grace;
Their shoes I need not wear in the first place
For your fire warms my heart without doubt
And I would not spite the flame with a pout.

LSS LXXXXIV

Blessed be this minute Lord that my pen draws
Conclusions to your mercy without flaws;
Warranting the heart of this world to beat
And spin round the sun which by your strength heat
And glue me to reflecting the bright light
You have lit at my feet to shine my way right
So I don't let fight or might smear Your sheen
By which gleam I gloss to push the foe green
With rage that gives him the darkness lesson
He wished to inflict on poor me for not
Abiding by his mean acts that prison
Hopeful souls that would see theirs come to naught.
Were I to drop after this resistance
Glory be to God for my persistence.

LSS LXXXXV

I've now come of age under your guidance
And Your Name doth shield me from resistance
Which at this point should have had me in tears
Drenched had I elected the warring spears
The devil uses to spill human blood
And quench his thirst but cannot steal Your spot.
With joy my heart burst and blooms forever
For Your Might rights the world of fever.
Heeding You fills me in with these sacred
Songs I've sung and of them make no secret
To enjoin the rest to seek with earnestness
Your great given gift for their happiness.
The fiend has been shamed and to his knees brought
Without fears by the faith You've in me wrought.

Printed in the United States
By Bookmasters